THE
FATHER'S
BLESSING

Devotional

JOSHUA & JODI YOUNG

The Father's Blessing Devotional

© Copyright 2015 by Streams Ministries International

Published by Streams Ministries International
www.streamsministries.com

Artwork and Design by Maria Martinez

ISBN: 978-0-9910409-9-5
Printed in the United States of America.

For additional information on this topic and other Streams Ministries resources, please visit our website:
www.streamsministries.com

FOR A FREE CATALOG OF STREAMS' BOOKS AND OTHER MATERIALS CALL
1-888-441-8080 (USA AND CANADA)
OR 817-354-5665

TABLE OF CONTENTS

THE FATHER'S BLESSING

"May the LORD bless you and keep you; The LORD
make His face shine upon you, and be gracious to you;
The LORD lift up His countenance upon you,
and give you peace."
Numbers 6:24-26

*And from me, from my heart, as a father, and a
grandfather, I'd like to bless you in this way:*

"May you reach the purpose for which you were
created. May you have courage above your peers.

May you have more passion for the things of God
than others think is necessary. May you dream more
than others think is practical.

May you expect more than others think is possible.
May you choose wisely, without earthly bias. You have
people to influence that you've not yet met; you have
lives to change that are waiting for your arrival. You
are strategically placed wherever God takes you, by
His grand design, just so you can become everything
He made you to be.

That place is the place you can grow best; that place
is the place where you can be most fruitful; the place

where the future is changed because of your presence. May you see vistas that others don't even know exist; may you see God in every petal of every flower, and in every blade of grass, for each of them are designed by His hand.

May you bless your children, and may they become giants in the faith under the mighty hand of God. You won't fail; you were made by God to be here— for such a time as this."

–John Paul Jackson

DECLARATIVE PRAYER

God has planted the seed of His Spirit inside you.
Every time you agree with Him about who you are,
that seed is fertilized and watered. The harvest field of
your life will spring forth, and in the right season and
in the right way, it will happen. Whatever you need to
accomplish God's purpose, God will do. He will move
Heaven and Earth to help you accomplish the purpose
for which you were created. These are the things the
Scripture says about you…

You are the light of the world because the Light of the
world dwells in you. You will bear God's light to change
the world. You will become increasingly aware of the
light of God that you carry. You will grow in God and
grow in His light. God's Kingdom will come and God's
will, will be done in you, as it is in Heaven. No one will
meet you and not be changed because of God's Spirit in
you. You will believe the unbelievable; what you are not
yet, you will become. You will come to understand who
you are in God, and soon, you will see your future more
clearly than ever before.

The gifts God has given you will begin to flourish as
you understand God's ways. Nothing will prosper that
comes against you, because you will live a repentant
life before God. You will become what God has called
you to become. You have been placed here for such
a time as this. You live where you live because God

placed you here. You're not here by accident; you're here by divine appointment. Your neighbors will prosper because of God in you. Where you work will prosper because of God in you. Those you touch will prosper because of God in you.

God's Spirit will flow through you. Therefore, it's impossible for you to pray for anyone and them not be touched. It makes no difference if they recognize it or not. God will touch them. God will touch others more at times than at other times. You will not judge your relationship with God based solely on what they feel. You relate to God because God's Spirit is in you and the blood of Jesus has covered you—not because of what others say, not because of your emotions, not because you feel saved, not because you've ascended to anything, but because of what God has done in you.

You're procreated, regenerated, and born anew. God's seed of light has entered you. Your spirit is alive and quickened because God's breath is in you. You will become quickened to God, fine-tuned to God's Spirit, not doing what God's not doing and doing what God is doing. You'll become a witness for God, because God's light in you proves to others that God exists. With God's help, when people see you, they will see the Father. Soon, there will be a clear distinction between those who don't know God and you, because you know God. People will look at you and they will know that you are a follower of Jesus and a bearer of His light. For God's glory, this will happen; taking the foolish things to confound the wise, all because you're growing closer to God.

–John Paul Jackson

BLESSING AND CURSING

"I am a blessed person. I have been given by God the ability to be blessed, and to be a blessing to others. I have been given by God the power to speak out these blessings in my life, and to see these blessings come to life. Every word that I speak can attract help from You, O God; help from Heaven. Every word I speak has the power to stop the effect of curses that I have spoken out, or that have been spoken over me; even curses that I've unknowingly spoken over me. Jesus, because You willingly took upon Yourself the curses of the world, I no longer have to live under the power of those curses.

And so, beginning right now, Holy Spirit, help me recognize every idle word that I speak. Help me to stop the power of that word instantly by believing and speaking the truth. I will believe, and I will speak the truth about myself. I will believe and speak the truth about others as well. In doing so, my life is going to change. Every area of my life will improve, because that's how You created me. You created me to be blessed, and to be a blessing to others—help me. Amen."

–John Paul Jackson

INTRODUCTION

In the deepest place of every human heart you will find a common thread connecting us all. If you listen carefully you'll hear a cry for acceptance and assurance that we are loved by someone who is greater than us.

As young children, when we need to be reminded of this reality, we simply stretch out our arms with great abandon knowing that our longing will soon be fulfilled. (If there is delay, then we simply make our request known a little louder.) As we are lifted up into our father's embrace, we experience a confidence and strength that quickly drives out any sign of fear or worry.

For some of you reading this, what I'm describing sounds like a fairytale, for you have never known that relationship with your earthly father. For others, while you have experienced the love of your earthly father, there comes a point in life when this assurance of acceptance no longer goes deep enough to comfort and strengthen the deepest places of your heart.

While the love and support of an earthly father is very important in our lives we will never fulfill the purpose for which we were created without receiving and walking in the blessing of our Heavenly Father. So whatever your story may be, today we are on a level playing field. We all need to experience the life-changing warmth of our Heavenly Father's embrace.

Many of us live our lives with a hope something will "happen" to us one day, magically making everything better. *If only the right person would come into my life. If I could just get a new job, or if they would just notice me...* and the list goes on. But what if the very thing that moves us forward in the purposes of God already exists in each of us? What if everything we need to step into His plan was spoken over us, deposited in us, even before the foundations of the earth?

The Heavenly Father's blessing is more than just words we read on a page. It's more than words spoken over us to make us feel better about life. It is His very breath, the wind of His Spirit, breathed over us. It's the same wind that was blowing in Acts 2 in the upper room, and the same wind that blew and parted the Red Sea, to make a way for the children of Israel to enter the Promised Land.

Every word Father God has spoken over you has literally formed something *in* you. We read in Genesis 1 that all of creation was spoken into existence by the words of God. His words of blessing over you are not meant to merely be an encouragement to you, but to literally create in you the very thing you need to walk in the purpose for which you were created. Can you hear them? Can you hear His words of blessing over you? Can you feel the glorious vibrations as the truth of your identity thunders over you?

In the fall of 1997, I began to feel those vibrations, and my perception and understanding of the Father was forever changed. My wife, Jodi, and I were living in Jacksonville, Florida, where we attended the Jacksonville Vineyard Christian Fellowship. I was one of the worship leaders there, and in a staff meeting I was told a prophet was coming to minister. All of my experiences with the prophetic to that point had been unhealthy to say the least. So to say I was skeptical was an understatement. The minister's name? John Paul Jackson.

When John Paul began to minister, I was blown away. He displayed such authority, but it was wrapped in love. Needless to say, our lives were radically touched that day. As John Paul ministered, both Jodi and I began to weep. He wasn't even speaking to us. We were just impacted by the anointing of God on his life and the wonderful weight of God's tangible presence in the room.

Growing up in the church, I had the opportunity to be around many amazing ministers of the gospel. While almost all of those experiences were beneficial and meaningful to me, there was something different about this one. This man spoke of God in ways I had never heard before. At the time I had been saved for over 16 years, but it was as if I was experiencing God for the first time. John Paul spoke of the Father with such awe and wonder.

After the service was over and most of the people had left, I stayed behind. As I paced back and forth on the stage, still shaken by the impact of that morning, I began to ask the Lord a question. *What was so different about this man?* I realized with most of the other ministers I had encountered, there was something about them I longed to have for myself. Maybe it was their ministry style, or their charisma, but with John Paul, it was different. I waited in silence for a few minutes, and then the answer came. As the thought entered my mind, without warning, I said it out loud, "I want to know God the way *he* knows God."

At the time I'm writing this, 18 years have passed since that day. I have been honored to spend most of that time connected with John Paul—planting churches, leading worship at conferences, searching out the ways and wonders of our God. I've been around through hard times and through some extremely good times. I know him as teacher, spiritual father, and friend. After all this time, when I think of John Paul, the same desire wells up in my heart—I want to know God the way he knows God.

John Paul is an example of how we as ordinary people can do extraordinary things when we know our God. One of the most important things we should know about God is that He is our Father and He wants us to walk in the power of His blessing. When our hearts are open to what God has spoken over us, and we begin to believe what He has established in us, nothing is impossible.

As you begin this three-week journey into *The Father's Blessing*, here are some questions to consider:

How do you see God? Who do you believe Him to be? Are your dreams limited by your own ability, or do you allow your heart to enter into the realm of faith it takes to grab hold of God-sized dreams?

This devotional is a tool to help you more fully understand and walk in the Father's blessing. Our thought life affects our belief, our belief determines our actions, and our actions produce the results that define our lives. If we have an accurate view of God and His blessing over us, before too long, our faith will increase along with the spiritual fruit in our lives.

I encourage you to open up your heart, take a deep breath, and allow the blessing of the Father to overtake you. This is your time.

– Joshua Young

WEEK 1:
WHAT IS THE BLESSING?

DAY 1

THE FATHER'S HEART

The first words God spoke to man and woman were words of blessing! Think of that! He had just created them from His own image, according to His likeness, and for His good pleasure. Out of all His affection, all of His love, and in accordance with His plans and purposes for mankind, He spoke:

> Then God blessed them, and God said to them, "Be fruitful and multiply; fill the earth and subdue it; have dominion over the fish of the sea, over the birds of the air, and over every living thing that moves on the earth."
>
> *Genesis 1:28*

The Hebrew word for blessing in this passage is *barak,* meaning to bless, kneel, or bend the knee. It also means to adore, praise, and salute. Understanding the definition of this word allows us to clearly see the picture Scripture is painting. It's one of someone kneeling down to make you great, and that is exactly what Father God did! From the very beginning, He knelt down from the heights of His majestic throne to make mankind great. In the garden, *every* aspect of their lives were blessed.

> He created them male and female, and blessed them and called them Mankind in the day they were created.
>
> *Genesis 5:2*

Today, just as He did with Adam and Eve, the Father still calls us by name, speaking words of blessing, and elevating us beyond what we could think, hope, or imagine. Scripture tells us we have been blessed with every spiritual blessing.

Praise be to the God and Father of our Lord Jesus Christ, who has blessed us in the heavenly realms with every spiritual blessing in Christ. For he chose us in him before the creation of the world to be holy and blameless in his sight. In love he predestined us for adoption to sonship through Jesus Christ, in accordance with his pleasure and will.

Ephesians 1:3-5 (NIV)

Before the foundation of the earth, the Father's blessing has gone before us. Like a spiritual compass, it helps us navigate life's pitfalls, and guides us on Heaven's path. However, even with this knowledge, one prevailing question still remains. Why? Why would the God who holds the universe in His hands bend down to make you and I great? Why would He even be mindful of us? The answer is simple—His great love for us! It brings the Father great pleasure to bless us as sons and daughters. We must never forget that. Also, you can't fulfill His will on earth—what He created you for—without it!

May you forever be conscious of the truth, that from the very beginning you have been blessed. Remember to always walk in the good way, and "you will find rest for your soul" (Jeremiah 6:16).

MEDITATION:

Reread the three scriptures again two more times. As you do, imagine the Father, the King and Creator, bending down to speak blessing over you.

Ask the Holy Spirit to speak to you about them and to pour out the love of the Father (Romans 5:5) as you read.

Read these verses again, but this time insert your name in place of the pronouns. Do this twice out loud. For example:

"Praise be to the God and Father of our Lord Jesus Christ, who has blessed Jodi in the heavenly realms with every spiritual blessing in Christ. For he chose Jodi in him before the creation of the world to be holy and blameless in his sight. In love he predestined Jodi for adoption to sonship through Jesus Christ, in accordance with his pleasure and will."

Listen to *The Father's Blessing* on CD or read it on page 4.

DAY 2
THE BLESSING OF ABRAHAM

Growing up in Sunday school we'd often sing a song titled, *Father Abraham*. You might remember some of the lyrics, "Father Abraham, had many sons, and many sons had father Abraham…" While today we know Abraham to be the father of many nations, when God first came to him, he was simply known as Abram, just an ordinary man living in a pagan city surrounded by idol worshippers, and married to a barren wife. His own father led his family to Haran from Ur with plans to go to Canaan, but never made it. He settled in Haran, and it was there he died.

From there God called Abram to a new place—a better place—a place God had ordained. Then He attached the blessing to him so his path would be blessed as he went. He had *everything* he needed to fulfill what God called him to. Not only were all of Abram's needs met, but the needs of his entire family line were met as well.

> Now the Lord had said to Abram: *"Get out of your country, from your family and from your father's house, to a land that I will show you. I will make you a great nation; I will bless you and make your name great; and you shall be a blessing. I will bless those who bless you, and I will curse him who curses you; and in you all the families of the earth shall be blessed."*
>
> Genesis 12:1-3 (KJV)

Abraham wasn't always the man we know today. In fact, when God first spoke to him, his life was a bit of a mess. Coming to the realization that God will call us and bless us right in the middle of our mess is key to receiving and walking in the blessing of the Lord. In the natural we often require visual proof before we judge something to be accurate. In other words, *seeing* is believing. But in the Kingdom of God, *belief* is what gives us spiritual sight to see. We will never be able to figure out the ways of God through the natural means of reasoning and logical thinking. What is required of us is to receive the blessing, and believe. We can't wait to go when we have everything figured out; the Father's blessing contains everything we need *to* figure it out. All we have to do in the middle of our mess is believe. This is what Abraham did. He believed God would do what He said and promised:

Abraham believed God, and it was accounted to him for righteousness.

Romans 4:3

Every time God spoke to him, he just simply believed. He took God at His word. He reckoned the one Who made the stars and everything on the planet could easily give him a child in his old age!

Then God said to Abraham, "As for Sarai your wife, you shall not call her name Sarai, but Sarah shall be her name. And I will bless her and also give you a son by her; then I will bless her, and she shall be a mother of nations; kings of peoples shall be from her." Then Abraham fell on his face and laughed, and said in his heart, "Shall a child be born to a man who is one hundred years old? And shall Sarah, who is ninety years old, bear a child?" And Abraham said to God, "Oh, that Ishmael might live before You!" Then God said: "No, Sarah your wife

*shall bear you a son, and you shall call his name Isaac; I
will establish My covenant with him for an everlasting
covenant, and with his descendants after him. And as
for Ishmael, I have heard you. Behold, I have blessed
him, and will make him fruitful, and will multiply
him exceedingly. He shall beget twelve princes, and I
will make him a great nation. But My covenant I will
establish with Isaac, whom Sarah shall bear to you at
this set time next year." Then He finished talking with
him, and God went up from Abraham.*

Genesis 17:15-22

When God spoke the blessing over Abraham's life, he believed it.
He knew how to hear and receive the Word with confidence and
assurance so that he walked in the blessing.

*And not being weak in faith, he did not consider his
own body, already dead (since he was about a hundred
years old), and the deadness of Sarah's womb. He did
not waver at the promise of God through unbelief, but
was strengthened in faith, giving glory to God, and
being fully convinced that what He had promised, He
was also able to perform.*

Romans 4:19-21

Abraham's story is an ancient one whose truth is still alive today.
Did you know that same blessing is available to you by faith?
His blessing is your blessing. You are his seed and heir, and have
a right to receive an inheritance. All you have to do is believe it!

*So then those who are of faith are blessed
with believing Abraham.*

Galatians 3:9

> And if you *are* Christ's, then you are Abraham's seed,
> and heirs according to the promise.
>
> Galatians 3:29

MEDITATION:

Abraham is called the "father of all who believe…" (Romans 4:11 NLT). When God spoke the blessing over him, he had a choice. Would he believe what God said or ignore it? Would he put his feet with his faith and step out in it? Or would he stay put in Haran?

Would he look at his circumstances or trust the Word?

We have a choice too. Ask the Lord to help you believe the words spoken. Belief is the very foundation of our faith. It is absolute trust in who God is, what He says, and where He is leading.

Belief is faith in the One who is faithful—confidence in the One that knows it all and created it all is able (Ephesians 3:20 and 2 Corinthians 9:8). Belief is convinced, despite circumstances, its hope is in a kind, good, loving Jesus instead of a circumstance. Abraham's circumstances didn't look great. He and his wife were old and unable to produce. He lived with a family most of his life that were quitters (Genesis 11:31). But, he believed God and stepped out.

Write down your not-so-great circumstances right now—the ones you seem to have no way to change—and present them to the Lord. Allow His truth to speak over your situation. Stay with the Word until you are convinced and unwavering in your trust in Him and what He says. Write it down and *believe* in your heart, and with your feet, what He says (James 2:14).

DAY 3
ASK AND RECEIVE!

Don't be afraid to ask for blessing. In fact, be bold! Jabez's life apparently started off poorly. So bad in fact, his mother cursed him with the name *Jabez*, meaning *sorrow* or *grief*. Determined that even though his starting place was full of sorrow and grief, it wouldn't be where he finished. He boldly asked the only One that could bend down and make "sorrow and grief" something great.

He asked God for a blessing, and that he would *not* do the thing he was named to do—cause pain. Because he asked, God granted what he requested. The phrase, 'You would bless me indeed," actually reads in Hebrew, "*barak, barak.*" He was asking for double for his trouble and God granted his bold request!

Now Jabez was more honorable than his brothers, and his mother called his name Jabez, saying, "Because I bore him in pain." And Jabez called on the God of Israel saying, "Oh, that You would bless me indeed, and enlarge my territory, that Your hand would be with me, and that You would keep me from evil, that I may not cause pain!" So God granted him what he requested.

1 Chronicles 4:9-10

In Jacob we see another example of someone boldly requesting the blessing of the Lord. As he was making his way back to his father's house after a fourteen-year absence, his future was uncertain, to say the least. His father-in-law had been chasing him most of the way, seeking the blessing on his life. The last time he had seen his family, his brother wanted to kill him. On top of all of that, in the middle of the night an angel came and wrestled with him. I don't know about you but wrestling with one of God's fiery ones doesn't sound easy! Nevertheless, Jacob held on even when the angel asked him to let go. He wouldn't let go until he blessed him. He knew his path needed to be blessed for the new season he was about to enter, so he boldly asked to be blessed. Who does that? He was tired, scared, worn out, and something rose up on the inside, "Bless me!" The angel did, and the blessing he released was a new name, "Israel." He changed his identity from Jacob (deceiver) to Israel (Prince with God).

Then Jacob was left alone; and a Man wrestled with him until the breaking of day. Now when He saw that He did not prevail against him, He touched the socket of his hip; and the socket of Jacob's hip was out of joint as He wrestled with him. And He said, "Let Me go, for the day breaks." But he said, "I will not let You go unless You bless me!" So He said to him, "What is your name?" He said, "Jacob." And He said, "Your name shall no longer be called Jacob, but Israel for you have struggled with God and with men, and have prevailed." Then Jacob asked, saying, "Tell me Your name, I pray." And He said, "Why is it that you ask about My name?" And He blessed him there.

Genesis 32:24-29

It doesn't matter who or what caused the difficulties you're facing today, or even the negative actions you've taken out on others because of your pain. What matters is the solution can only be found in the One who can turn the situation totally around. Be bold! Ask to be blessed! See how God grants your request and changes your circumstances and turns everything around!

MEDITATION:

Read over the two verses again.

Can you relate to Jabez or Jacob? Maybe your life hasn't gone the way you wanted.

Meditate on the two Scriptures. Speak the words. Imagine the words.

Listen to see if the Lord changes your name.

Finish your meditation time by asking the Lord to bless you indeed–*barak, barak*. Then lift your hands up to heaven and receive from the Lord. *"For everyone who asks, receives..."* (Luke 11:10).

Listen to *Blessing and Cursing* on CD or read it on page 8.

DAY 4
COMMANDED BLESSING

There is power in the Name. He is Mighty God, Warrior, Lord of Hosts. We see a picture of God that is powerful, mighty, strong, and triumphant in battle. When this all-powerful God gives a command, it is done! Angels take to flight, the waves part, the mountains bow down. The Lord's command is always accomplished!

...the Lord commanded the blessing—Life forevermore.

Psalm 133:3 (KJV)

When the Commander-in-Chief gives a command, those under him obey. They plan and execute the orders of the high-ranking officer.

God commanded the blessing over you! His Word does not return void. It will do what it was sent to do. Nothing, and no one can change the command of the King!

When Balak hired Balaam to curse the Israelites, he couldn't do it. Balaam declared in Numbers 23:19-20:

> *God is not a man, that He should lie, nor a son of man, that He should repent. Has He said, and will He not do? Or has He spoken, and will He not make it good? Behold, I have received a command to bless; He has blessed, and I cannot reverse it.*

God had already blessed Israel. Nothing anyone could say would change that. It was done!

Abraham knew the promise of God:

> *I will bless those who bless you, and I will curse him who curses you...*
>
> Genesis 12:3

He didn't have to worry about what people said or did because Mighty God would take care of it. People could talk about him, lie, cheat, and steal, but the Lord of Hosts would take care of it, and he would come out blessed.

Remember, there is no reason to worry or fret. The Warrior is on your side, and He has already spoken!

MEDITATION:

Have you been worried or anxious about what others have said about you? Have you thought how their words will affect your future at work, church, or family relationships?

Look up the following verses: Deuteronomy 28:8, Isaiah 54:16-17, Psalm 103:20, Psalm 37:1-4.

What is the truth of God for this situation?

Listen to the *Declarative Prayer* on CD, or read it on page 6 and decide to declare the truth.

DAY 5
PAINT A PICTURE

When Jacob and Esau were born to Isaac and Rebekah, the blessing had been in operation in Abraham's family line for two generations. When God speaks a thing it doesn't return void!

So shall My word be that goes forth from My mouth;
It shall not return to Me void, But it shall accomplish
what I please, and it shall prosper in the thing for which
I sent it.

Isaiah 55:11

Isaac was near death and knew the power of God's Word, so he planned to bless his first-born son. Also knowing the potency of blessing, Rebekah planned for Jacob to get the blessing instead. Isaac spoke an amazing word picture over Jacob's path which showed him clearly what his future would look like:

And he came near and kissed him; and he smelled the
smell of his clothing, and blessed him and said: "Surely,
the smell of my son is like the smell of a field which the
Lord has blessed. Therefore may God give you of the
dew of heaven, of the fatness of the earth, and plenty of
grain and wine. Let peoples serve you, and nations bow
down to you. Be master over your brethren, and let your

> mother's sons bow down to you. Cursed *be* everyone who
> curses you, and blessed *be* those who bless you!"

Genesis 27:27-30

Later, as Jacob prepared to leave on a journey to find his wife, Isaac declared this over his son:

> May God Almighty bless you, and make you fruitful
> and multiply you, That you may be an assembly
> of peoples; and give you the blessing of Abraham,
> to you and your descendants with you, that you
> may inherit the land in which you are a stranger,
> which God gave to Abraham.

Genesis 28: 3-4

When speaking the blessing, we must give a clear, concise visualization of what the receiver's life will be like with the blessing—painting a beautiful picture of the future with artistic words as color and skillful strokes of a defined, good life.

MEDITATION:

Read the whole account of Jacob and Esau's blessing in Genesis 27-28.

Take note that the blessing is *always* spoken when it is pronounced. This is Isaiah 55:11. Why is this?

What kind of picture did Isaac paint of Jacob's future with his words? Underline the areas of Jacob's life the blessing included.

Listen to *The Father's Blessing* on CD or read it on page 4.

Allow the words to paint a picture of your future. As you listen to this blessing, begin to identify and visualize the areas of your life the Lord wants to unlock and bring into focus.

DAY 6
THE BLESSING IS FINANCIAL

The blessing covers so much of a person's life. God kneels down to make you great and empower you to succeed. Part of that empowering is to bless you with what you need financially to do what God has ordained. When God called Abraham to go to a land he did not know, He told him, "Fear not, Abram, I am your Shield, your abundant compensation, and your reward shall be exceedingly great" (Genesis 15:1 AMP). Basically He was saying, *Don't fear, I'll be your BIG paycheck. You don't have to worry about finances.* Isn't this exactly what Jesus exhorted us to do—to not worry about our lives, but seek first the Kingdom of God and His righteousness? (Matthew 6:25-34)

But without faith it is impossible to please Him, for he who comes to God must believe that He is, and that He is a rewarder of those who diligently seek Him.

Hebrews 11:6

There has been so much false teaching and deception in the area of Kingdom finances. We have to wash our mind with the Word of God and walk in the Truth of what He says, He is, was, and will be *Jehovah Jireh*— the God who sees what you need and will provide—especially when you are seeking to do His will. When you understand the true meaning of His name, you realize that a God who created you with a perfect plan will provide all you need to accomplish His will.

The blessing of the Lord makes one rich, and He adds no sorrow with it.

Proverbs 10:22

When God revealed Himself as *Jehovah Jireh* to Abraham, He had called him to a test.

Take now your son, your only son Isaac, whom you love, and go to the land of Moriah, and offer him there as a burnt offering on one of the mountains of which I shall tell you.

Genesis 22:2

In the test, God provided the answer—the ram instead of Isaac. God always provides for you when He calls you!

MEDITATION:

Have you been fearful concerning finances?

Have you been afraid to step out on the path God is calling you to because you aren't sure about a paycheck?

God is your source and your abundant compensation; you don't need to fear!

Put the Word in your heart about God being your source of blessing by memorizing the above verses.

Make a list of everything you would do if money wasn't an issue.

Now ask God what He is calling you to do right now. God always pays for what He cooks up.

For more on God's provision, study: Genesis 24:25; Deuteronomy 28:11-12; Genesis 24:1; Matthew 6:25-34; Malachi 3:10.

DAY 7
BLESS THE LORD

O ver the last few days, we have learned "to bless" is to kneel down, praise, salute, make happy and straight. Over and over again in Scripture we see God blessing His children. Our response to God's loving-kindness, goodness, and graciousness is to bless Him right back—praise Him ... bless Him ... salute Him ... kneel before Him ... magnify Him.

Oh, bless our God, you peoples and make the voice of His praise to be heard.

Psalm 66:8

Blessed be the Lord, who daily loads us with benefits, the God of our salvation!

Psalm 68:19

Oh come, let us worship and bow down; let us kneel before the Lord our Maker.

Psalm 95:6

One of the most difficult times to do this is in the face of adversity. In hard times, our emotions take over and we start to focus on and talk about the problem. Knowing our human tendencies, David learned to make his soul (mind, will, and emotions) bless the Lord. Making a choice to surrender our soul (mind, will, and emotions) to the King of Kings in the midst of hardship will drastically change our perspective:

> *Bless the Lord, O my soul; and all that is within me, bless His holy name! Bless the Lord, O my soul, and forget not all His benefits.*
>
> Psalm 103:1-2

> *Bless the Lord, O my soul! O Lord my God, You are very great: You are clothed with honor and majesty.*
>
> Psalm 104:1

We must remember in these times we *are* His children. And as children, we don't have to understand all the details of the situation; we just have to trust in the Father.

He *has been* kind, good, generous, and loving.

He *is* kind, good, generous, and loving right now in the midst of whatever is going on.

He *will be* kind, good, generous, and loving because He changes not.

In 2 Chronicles 20 we come upon King Jehoshaphat during a tremendously difficult time. Jehoshaphat and all of Judah faced an impossible situation. Three armies were coming to attack them, and in the natural, there was no way to win. Faced with a desperate reality, Jehoshaphat made the choice to lift up his soul to the Lord and not get discouraged. He called a fast and lifted up his eyes to the Maker of Heaven. He sent the musicians into battle first, blessing the Lord, and singing of His love that endures forever. In the end, the three armies turned on themselves. When Judah arrived to fight, their enemies had all been destroyed!

Instead of fighting, they plundered and praised for three days, choosing to name the place *The Valley of Blessing*.

Learn to trust and praise Him on the mountaintops and in the valleys. You are blessed wherever you are. Don't get discouraged—just look to Him. Get low and look up!

And on the fourth day they assembled in the Valley of Berachah, for there they blessed the Lord; therefore the name of that place was called The Valley of Berachah until this day.

2 Chronicles 20:26

MEDITATION:

No matter what you are going through right now, you can do all things through Christ who gives you strength! He is with you and will give you wisdom, comfort, and guidance.

Choose to bless the Lord with your soul! You might need to get on the floor and bend your knees to Him and raise your hands while with one voice you praise Him.

Choose to name the valley you are in *The Valley of Blessing*, where you are going to bless His name until the victory comes!

For further study, read: 1 Chronicles 20; Psalm 23; Psalm 103.

WEEK 2:
RECEIVE THE BLESSING

DAY 8
LEADERS THAT BLESS

A leader is someone who leads, out in front, showing the people the right way to go. God shows us through His Word what spiritual leaders are to do. Part of their job is to bless—empower others to succeed. As Melchizedek did Abram:

And he blessed him and said: "Blessed be Abram of God Most High, Possessor of heaven and earth...

Genesis 14:19

...but because Jesus lives forever, he has a permanent priesthood. Therefore he is able to save completely those who come to God through him, because he always lives to intercede for them.

Hebrews 7:24-25 NIV

God told Moses that part of the priests' job was to speak blessing:

"Speak to Aaron and his sons, saying, 'This is the way you shall bless the children of Israel. Say to them: "The Lord bless you and keep you; The Lord make His face shine upon you, And be gracious to you; The Lord lift up His countenance upon you, And give you peace."' *"So they shall put My name on the children of Israel, and I will bless them."*

Numbers 6:23-27

The priests' blessing initiated change in people's future:

> *And Eli would bless Elkanah and his wife, and say,*
> *"The Lord give you descendants from this woman for*
> *the loan that was given to the Lord." Then they would*
> *go to their own home.*
>
> 1 Samuel 2:20

One of the reasons *The Father's Blessing* by John Paul Jackson is so powerful is that it comes from one of God's spiritual leaders rightfully doing his job—serving the people by speaking blessing. God puts spiritual leaders in our lives to train, equip, challenge, correct, and show us the way to go. Some of us don't have spiritual leaders in our lives who can do these things. Listen to *The Father's Blessing* on CD or read it on page 4 and allow the blessing to empower you to succeed, prosper, and initiate change with the anointing of a spiritual leader's blessing.

MEDITATION:

Think of as many biblical leaders you can who have blessed. Write them down now.

Read over Numbers 6:23-27 two times. Why would God want the priests to speak this over the Israelites regularly?

Why is it important to hear the blessing regularly?

DIGGING DEEPER:

Are you a spiritual leader? Make sure you are speaking blessings over your people consistently.

For further study, read: Hebrews 5:6; Hebrews 2:17; 2 Samuel 6:18.

DAY 9
YOUR FUTURE LOOKS BLESSED

What I love about John Paul Jackson's *The Father's Blessing* is that he speaks a future for the listener—exactly what the blessing of the father is supposed to do. True fathers have the prophetic capability to see your future and make it clear to you by spoken word. They see you in light of who God created you to be, even though at the moment you may not be walking in that reality. They capture a glimpse of your destiny and make it clear to you, even propelling you in the way you should go. This is what Jacob did for his twelve sons.

> *Jacob called his sons and said, "Gather around. I want to tell you what you can expect in the days to come."*
>
> *Genesis 49:1 (MSG)*

Jacob had seen the future and was telling them what they were going to encounter and meet on their path.

The Hebrew word used for "tell" is *nagad*, meaning announce, report, messenger, to be in front of, or in sight. Jacob was a prophetic messenger reporting what he had seen in front of them. He called them all together to announce the future, positioning them to begin to look for and expect blessing along the way.

WOW! That is the power of a father's blessing on full display.

> For I know the thoughts that I think toward you, says
> the Lord, thoughts of peace and not of evil, to give you
> a future and a hope.
>
> Jeremiah 29:11

As sons and daughters of God, our paths are paved with the blessings of Heaven. The boundaries and conditions of our future are certain, the plan for our life is known by God, and He orders our steps (Proverbs 16:9).

Before Jacob begins to speak the future, he says:

> Gather together and hear, you sons of Jacob, and listen
> to Israel your father.
>
> Genesis 49:2

The words hear and listen are actually the same word in Hebrew, *shama*, meaning hear, listen, yield, obey. He wanted his children to hear it, *really* hear what he was saying—so it would become a part of them. Then their actions would come into alignment with this reality.

Your future is blessed. This is your reality, but will you hear it, believe it, yield to it, and act on it? Never allow life's circumstances to distract you and prevent you from walking in the Father's blessing.

MEDITATION:

Listen to *The Father's Blessing* on CD or read it on page 4. Allow John Paul to be a prophetic messenger reporting what is in front of you. *Shama, Shama* what he is telling you. In other words, *really* hear, so that you may obey.

DAY 10
WHAT TO LOOK FOR

When the Israelites were getting ready to enter the Promised Land, God wanted them to know what to expect. He gave them a declaration in Deuteronomy 28 that basically said, *This is what is going to happen. These blessings shall come on you and overtake you. Expect to be blessed in every area.* God, making the vision clear, built anticipation in the hearts of His people. It gave them something to look forward to, anticipate, and know if God said it, it would occur. It gave them eyes for their future—filled with good things.

When is the last time you talked with God about your future? Taking time to dream with God will bring clarity into your life and hope to your heart. Remember, the things God has prepared for you go beyond what you can think, hope, or even imagine. To get a full picture of His plan for your life requires you to cooperate with Him. Walking in the fullness of the Father's blessing requires us to believe, and step out in faith, beyond our own understanding and experiences. To get to places we've never been we must journey down untraveled roads.

Today, read Deuteronomy 28 and begin to dream with God. Allow him to make the vision of your future clear to your heart. Ask Him in what ways He desires to bless you. Remember the blessing is tangible! It comes on you! It overtakes you! Selah.

Now it shall come to pass, if you diligently obey the voice of the Lord your God, to observe carefully all His commandments which I command you today, that the Lord your God will set you high above all nations of the earth. And all these blessings shall come upon you and overtake you, because you obey the voice of the Lord your God: "Blessed shall you be in the city, and blessed shall you be in the country. Blessed shall be the fruit of your body, the produce of your ground and the increase of your herds, the increase of your cattle and the offspring of your flocks. Blessed shall be your basket and your kneading bowl. Blessed shall you be when you come in, and blessed shall you be when you go out. The Lord will cause your enemies who rise against you to be defeated before your face; they shall come out against you one way and flee before you seven ways. The Lord will command the blessing on you in your storehouses and in all to which you set your hand, and He will bless you in the land which the Lord your God is giving you. The Lord will establish you as a holy people to Himself, just as He has sworn to you, if you keep the commandments of the Lord your God and walk in His ways. Then all peoples of the earth shall see that you are called by the name of the Lord, and they shall be afraid of you. And the Lord will grant you plenty of goods, in the fruit of your body, in the increase of your livestock, and in the produce of your ground, in the land of which the Lord swore to your fathers to give you. The Lord will open to you His good treasure, the heavens, to give the rain to your land in its season, and to bless all the work of your hand. You shall lend to many nations, but you shall not borrow. And the Lord will make you the head and not the tail; you shall be above only, and not be beneath, if you heed the commandments of the Lord your God, which I command you today, and are careful *to observe them. So you shall not turn aside from any of the words which I command you this day, to the right or the left, to go after other gods to serve them."*

Deuteronomy 28: 1-14

Look at everything the blessing includes:

- You
- Your generations
- Your land
- Your belongings—everything you have
- Whatever you do—what you touch with your hands or your feet
- Wherever you are—it goes with you

MEDITATION:

Reread Deuteronomy 28:1-14. What stands out to you? Write it down.

Read it again and visualize it. Picture the blessing, receiving eyes for your future.

Listen to the *Declarative Prayer* on CD or read it on page 6.

CHALLENGE:

Memorize a verse a day from Deuteronomy 28 over the next 14 days.

DAY 11
A NEW NAME

Names are very important in the Bible. The naming of a child was the first declaration of blessing over that child's life. The mindset was that the meaning of your name set the course of your life (see Jabez, Benjamin, John the Baptist, and Jesus). When Leah named her son, she pronounced a blessing on him:

Then Leah said, "I am happy, for the daughters will call me blessed." So she called his name Asher.

Genesis 30:13

Ashar is one of the Hebrew words for blessed, and means:

- To be straight
- To be successful, prosper, fortunate
- To lead on
- Set right
- Advance
- Guide or lead straight
- Pronounce Happy
- Blessed

Ashar is the root word for each one of Leah's words above (Genesis 30). She was happy (adjective). People would call her happy (noun or adjective). Her son was named Happy (noun).

When you receive the blessing, this is your path—your identity! You are blessed and your path is set straight. Everything you do, everywhere you go, and everything you touch is successful and prosperous. That is your reality.

When walking in the blessing, others see it and want it. It looks good—a straight, prosperous, happy life! Leah knew others would see how blessed she was, so she named her child accordingly. Others experienced similar encounters. Laban saw how blessed Abraham's servant was and invited him to his home (Genesis 24:31). Abimelech wanted a covenant with Abraham because he saw his success and wanted it (Genesis 26:29). Even Pharaoh asked Moses to bless him because he saw the blessing (Exodus 12:32).

You may be thinking, *I don't feel that way.* If that's the case, allow the Father's blessing to change your name. On previous days, we talked about Abram. His name was changed by God to Abraham, "The Father of Many Nations," but that wasn't the only time an encounter with God required a name change.

Saul of Tarsus had a radical encounter with God on the road to Damascus, and was forever changed. God changed his name from Saul to Paul. He went from living a life where his main job description was persecuting Christians, to playing a key role in establishing the Church.

Simon was a rough, weathered fisherman when he encountered Jesus, who revealed to him his true purpose, and his name was changed to Peter (the Rock). Peter's destiny would then become the rock on which the Church was to be established. This required a name change.

Remember our circumstances do not determine our identity; rather our identity defines our circumstances. Greater is He who is in you than he who is in the world (1 John 4:4).

You are blessed to live a happy, joy-filled life (John 10:10). When you know that is your reality and begin to walk in it, others will begin to notice and want to experience the same transformation you've found.

MEDITATION:

Think about and write down the times others have taken note of your blessed life.

Look around you and begin to thank God for how He has blessed you—naming ten different ways you are blessed TODAY.

Read about biblical name changes (Genesis 17, Acts 13:9, Matthew 16:15-2).

There is always a reason for a biblical name change. Ask the Lord if you need a name change. What did He say and why?

DAY 12
AGREEMENT

The truth of the blessing will set you free! His Word will divide the soul (mind, will, and emotions) and the spirit, and judge correctly your thoughts and actions. Now you are ready to walk in it. But Amos tells us:

> *Can two walk together, unless they are agreed?*
>
> Amos 3:3

There is power in agreement! Jesus tells us:

> *Again I say to you that if two of you agree on earth concerning anything that they ask, it will be done for them by My Father in heaven.*
>
> Matthew 18:19

The word Jesus uses for agree is *symphōneō*. It is the Greek word from which we get *symphony*—meaning sound together, or to be in accord. There is a beautiful sound when we agree. If you aren't in agreement then there is division, doubt, and strife—that definitely sounds like something too—muttering, anxiety, shouting. We want to make sure we are always agreeing with the Lord and not agreeing with man, or worse yet, the enemy.

We hear His Word, then we agree with His Word. This is called believing. It is an eighteen-inch journey from our mind to our heart. Belief means nothing can convince us His Word is not true, because He is faithful and true. That eighteen-inch journey is incredibly important. Just because you *hear* doesn't mean you get it. I can hear a lecture on molecular physics but not understand a thing. This is the whole point of the Parable of the Sower:

> *But he who received seed on the good ground is he who hears the word and understands it, who indeed bears fruit and produces: some a hundredfold, some sixty, some thirty.*
>
> Matthew 13:23

Each time that you listen to *The Father's Blessing* CD or read the devotional make sure you haven't just heard, but you understand and agree. There is power when you agree with God's Word. In that place, belief will arise.

> *...as you have believed, so let it be done for you...*
>
> Matthew 8:13

We have to renew our mind to what God says. Review this devotion and the verses listed often. Write out the verses and commit them to memory. Read them out loud because faith comes by hearing. Here is a simple way to get into agreement. Since we know all scripture is God breathed and true, declare the following over Scripture:

- "Your Word says...."
- "I agree with it!"
- "Therefore, I believe in my heart and declare with my mouth the truth."

MEDITATION:

Listen to the *Declarative Prayer* on CD or read it on page 6. Allow the words to penetrate your heart and mind.

Do you *really* understand what He is saying?

Do you really agree with what He said?

Do you believe it? Did it make that eighteen–inch journey?

Now boldly declare *this prayer* out loud!.

DAY 13
EXPECT IT!

Faith and fear are opposite sides of the same coin. Both are the expectation something which hasn't happened yet is going to happen. Fear is the expectation something *bad* is going to happen, while faith is the expectation something *good* is going to happen. So the question is, what are you expecting?

God's plan has always been to bless. From the beginning of time, His desire has been to shower His best on His creation. Expecting bad things from a good God just doesn't make sense. We have to be willing to allow God to transform our mindset from one of walking in fear and dread to one that declares, *I'm receiving all you have stored up for me!*

I know what I'm doing. I have it all planned out—plans to take care of you, not abandon you, plans to give you the future you hope for.

Jeremiah 29:11 (MSG)

If God's plan is to bless you, then shouldn't you be living your life in great expectation of its arrival? What an amazing comfort to know you will never walk alone, and He will never leave you or forsake you. His desire is to shower you with His best, so look for it, and receive it!

When you know, really know, that your life has been blessed, you expect good things for your future. Here are some more verses which speak of our future in Christ.

He predestined us for adoption to sonship through Jesus Christ, in accordance with his pleasure and will.

Ephesians 1:5 (NIV)

Furthermore, because we are united with Christ, we have received an inheritance from God, for he chose us in advance, and he makes everything work out according to his plan.

Ephesians 1:11 (NLT)

For we are his workmanship, created in Christ Jesus unto good works, which God hath before ordained that we should walk in them.

Ephesians 2:10 (KJV)

Our expectation is based upon our belief of what the future holds, and really what we believe about God. While Scripture tells us we will experience trials and persecution, our salvation is based on Christ Jesus' finished work of the Cross, giving us access to the Father. Nothing can separate us from that reality. He is our future—such good news!

It's because of this reality that the woman of Proverbs 31 can "laugh without fear of the future." Our job is to walk on the blessed path, one step at a time. He will clear the path and make a way for us.

MEDITATION:

Reread each of the preceeding Scriptures. Write them on your heart, knowing God has a plan and He *will* accomplish His plan.

Ask the Holy Spirit to reveal areas of your life where you have been expecting evil to prevail in your future. Write down what He reveals.

Laugh at the future knowing God will work out all things for your good.

DAY 14

BLESSING PASSED DOWN

Legacy is important to all of us, and its importance grows with each passing year. What kind of impact will we have on the next generation? How can we make our ceiling (our stopping place) become our children's floor (their starting place)? Receiving and walking in the Father's blessing has greater impact than we might realize. The name-changing nature of God's spoken word over us can redefine a family line, and set up the next generation for great success.

Abram received the Heavenly Father's blessing, and walked it out. His whole life gave testimony of that blessing, and he became great just as his Father had declared he would. As his new name reflected, Abraham, "Father of Nations," God's blessing wouldn't stop when he died. The blessing would stretch beyond the borders of his lifetime, bequeathed to the generations to come. The momentum of God's word cannot be stopped. It continues to seek out the generations, doing what it was created to do—empowering them to succeed.

And it came to pass, after the death of Abraham, that God blessed his son Isaac. And Isaac dwelt at Beer Lahai Roi.

Genesis 25:11

There was a famine in the land, besides the first famine that was in the days of Abraham. And Isaac went to Abimelech king of the Philistines, in Gerar. Then the Lord appeared to him and said: "Do not go down to Egypt; live in the land of which I shall tell you. Dwell in this land, and I will be with you and bless you; for to you and your descendants I give all these lands, and I will perform the oath which I swore to Abraham your father. And I will make your descendants multiply as the stars of heaven; I will give to your descendants all these lands; and in your seed all the nations of the earth shall be blessed;…Then Isaac sowed in that land, and reaped in the same year a hundredfold; and the Lord blessed him.

Genesis 26:1-4; 12

And the Lord appeared to him the same night and said, "I am the God of your father Abraham; do not fear, for I am with you. I will bless you and multiply your descendants for My servant Abraham's sake."

Genesis 26:24

The blessing is passed down, not by human performance or will, but by the power and potency of the spoken Word of the Father. You can't earn the blessing; it is the Father's graciousness, and abounding love reaching down to make you great because you are His. It is in your family line, a family trait, to be blessed:

So then those who are of faith are blessed with believing Abraham.

Galatians 3:9

And if you are Christ's, then you are Abraham's seed,
and heirs according to the promise.

Galatians 3:29

You can't escape the blessing. It keeps chasing you down (Psalm 23:6). But it's not just you that is blessed, but all the generations in you!

As you continue to be awakened to all the Father's blessing holds, begin to talk about it with your natural and spiritual children. Speak over them the blessings of our Heavenly Father, and watch as a spiritual momentum grows in them to become an unstoppable force for the Kingdom.

MEDITATION:

Underline the areas the blessing included for Isaac in the three verses mentioned earlier in this chapter.

Notice in Genesis 26:24, God starts with, "I *am* the God of your father Abraham…"

Isaac had seen the blessing on his father's life just like others had. Then God says, "do not fear, for I *am* with you. I will bless you and multiply your descendants for My servant Abraham's sake." God displaces the fear of the famine with the fact that He (*Jehovah Jireh*) is with him.

Read Genesis 26:24 again two more times. Remember *you* are Abraham's seed (Galatians 3:9; 29). Insert your name into the verse and declare it out loud:

And the Lord appeared to _____ the same night and said, "I *am* the God of your father Abraham; do not fear, for

I *am* with _____. I will bless _____ and multiply ___
descendants for My servant Abraham's sake."

You are blessed not because of what you do, but because
of the power and potency of the blessing! The world's
circumstances don't matter to you; you're walking in the
blessing passed down from the Father!

WEEK 3:
WALK IN THE BLESSING

DAY 15
THE CHOICE IS YOURS

In Genesis 27 we read the story of Jacob and Esau. As the story unfolds, we see their mother Rebekah's plan for Jacob to obtain their father Issac's blessing through deception. This created family strife. How many times in our lives do we try to gain an advantage by unrighteous means? Lying, cheating on our taxes, or maybe talking about someone behind their back?

In the story, the blessing was already on them both, because it was a generational blessing from Abraham. They didn't have to plot, plan, or deceive to get it; it was already theirs from God's promise to their grandfather!

Each of Isaac's sons had a choice whether they would walk in truth and value the blessing of God. Jacob chose to obey his father and step out in the future that Isaac declared for him. However, Esau chose to do the opposite! He didn't value the blessing and the paths of these two brothers diverged at that point—one a blessed path and one not.

Esau saw that Isaac had blessed Jacob and sent him away to Padan Aram to take himself a wife from there, and that as he blessed him he gave him a charge, saying, "You shall not take a wife from the daughters of Canaan," and that Jacob had obeyed his father and his mother and had gone to Padan Aram. Also Esau saw that the daughters of Canaan did not please his father

> *Isaac. So Esau went to Ishmael and took Mahalath the daughter of Ishmael, Abraham's son, the sister of Nebajoth, to be his wife in addition to the wives he had.*
>
> Genesis 28:6-9

Because Jacob chose correctly (even though he had lied and cheated to get where he was) God came to him with the blessing and changed his name from Jacob (Deceiver) to Israel (Prince with God).

> *I am the Lord God of Abraham your father and the God of Isaac; the land on which you lie I will give to you and your descendants. Also your descendants shall be as the dust of the earth; you shall spread abroad to the west and the east, to the north and the south; and in you and in your seed all the families of the earth shall be blessed. Behold, I am with you and will keep you wherever you go, and will bring you back to this land; for I will not leave you until I have done what I have spoken to you.*
>
> Genesis 28:13-15

> *Then God appeared to Jacob again, when he came from Padan Aram, and blessed him. And God said to him, 'Your name is Jacob; your name shall not be called Jacob anymore, but Israel shall be your name.' So He called his name Israel. Also God said to him: 'I am God Almighty. Be fruitful and multiply; a nation and a company of nations shall proceed from you, and kings shall come from your body. The land which I gave Abraham and Isaac I give to you; and to your descendants after you I give this land.' Then God went up from him in the place where He talked with him. So Jacob set up a pillar in the place where*

> *He talked with him, a pillar of stone; and he poured*
> *a drink offering on it, and he poured oil on it. And*
> *Jacob called the name of the place where God spoke*
> *with him, Bethel.*
>
> Genesis 35:9-15

The book of Proverbs tells us to "Guard your heart above all else, for it determines the course of your life" (Proverbs 4:23 NLT). When our heart is full of fear, envy, and self-seeking, we fall into deception. Therefore, we take steps not in line with God's will.

> *See, I have set before you today life and good, death*
> *and evil, in that I command you today to love the*
> *Lord your God, to walk in His ways, and to keep His*
> *commandments, His statutes, and His judgments, that*
> *you may live and multiply; and the Lord your God*
> *will bless you in the land which you go to possess. But*
> *if your heart turns away so that you do not hear, and*
> *are drawn away… I have set before you life and death,*
> *blessing and cursing; therefore choose life…"*
>
> Deuteronomy 30:15-17, 19

God desires "truth in the inward parts," but in our hidden part He will help us to know wisdom (Psalm 51:6 KJV).

MEDITATION:

Have you been *trying* to get the blessing? You can tell if you are in "trying" mode by the fruit being produced—strife, deception, anger, lying, self-seeking.

Today is the day you can stop striving to get what your Heavenly Father is waiting to give you freely!

Like David, ask the Lord right now to search your heart and test your thoughts (Psalm 139:23).

Ask for your inner being to delight in God's law (Romans 7:22).

Write down what the Holy Spirit reveals and ask Him to help you walk on His *already* blessed path.

Allow the peace of God to come and guard your heart and mind (Philippians 4: 7). Enjoy the peace.

Pray Ephesians 3:16-21:

He would grant you, according to the riches of His glory, to be strengthened with might through His Spirit in the inner man, that Christ may dwell in your hearts through faith; that you, being rooted and grounded in love, may be able to comprehend with all the saints what is the width and length and depth and height—to know the love of Christ which passes knowledge; that you may be filled with all the fullness of God. Now to Him who is able to do exceedingly abundantly above all that we ask or think, according to the power that works in us...

Listen to *The Father's Blessing* on CD or read it on page 4 with a pure heart.

For further study: Deuteronomy 30:15-20; Proverbs 16:9; James 3:14-18; Luke 10:27; Genesis 27.

DAY 16
OVERFLOWING

The 1924 Olympic Games hosted in Paris, France, became the backdrop for Scottish–born runner, Eric Liddell, to take home the gold medal in the men's 400 meters. In 1981, his story made it to the big screen with the release of *Chariots of Fire*.

There is a scene in the movie where Eric and his sister, Jenny, are walking across the Scottish Highlands. Jenny is trying to convince Eric to return to China to take over the mission where their parents worked. In her opinion, it needed to be sooner than later. In a dramatic moment, Eric stops, turns to his sister and says, "Jenny I believe that God made me for a purpose, for China, but He also made me fast and when I run I feel His pleasure."[1] The motivation for Eric's running was to experience the pleasure of God. All of his athletic achievements, the races won making headlines for his country, the gold medals for Scotland, were the overflow of a life dedicated to pursuing the pleasure of God.

The same can be said about the blessing of God on your life. Simply receiving and walking in the Father's blessing positions you to impact those around you, even your country, as you pursue the presence and pleasure of God.

The abundance that pours forth from your life, and spills on to others around you is directly connected to the blessing of Abraham in Genesis 12:3.

---

[1] Chariots of Fire, DVD, directed by Hugh Hudson (1981; Burbank, CA: Warner Home Video, 2011).

> *I will bless those who bless you, And I will curse him who curses you; and in you all the families of the earth shall be blessed.*

You are a blessing agent for God on earth. The blessing is uncontainable! Wherever you go, whatever you do, whoever you touch gets blessed! Our mindset needs to be, *Here I am, watch out for the overflow!*

That is an exciting prospect when it's people we like, but what about the people we don't like, such as a crazy relative or a mean boss?

Jacob's life was so blessed that his lying father-in-law got blessed in the process:

> *And Laban said to him, "Please stay, if I have found favor in your eyes, for I have learned by experience that the Lord has blessed me for your sake." For what you had before I came was little, and it has increased to a great amount; the Lord has blessed you since my coming. And now, when shall I also provide for my own house?"*
>
> Genesis 30:27; 30

Joseph was a slave in Potiphar's house and because of the blessing the whole house and field of Potiphar was blessed.

> *So it was, from the time that he had made him overseer of his house and all that he had, that the Lord blessed the Egyptian's house for Joseph's sake; and the blessing of the Lord was on all that he had in the house and in the field.*
>
> Genesis 39:5

Today, know that you are an atmosphere shifter. You are literally a world changer. Remember, wherever you go, you bring the blessing of the Father with you. The overflow of your life will influence the world around you, and you will reach the purpose for which you where created.

MEDITATION:

Ask the Lord to make you aware of the blessing that is overflowing to others because of you. Notice how restaurants are suddenly full because you came in five minutes before. Watch how the business you work for suddenly has increased sales.

If you haven't realized by now… the blessing is on you! It is a part of who you are and what you look like to the world.

Salvation belongeth unto the LORD: thy blessing is upon thy people. Selah.

———— Psalm 3:8 (KJV) ————

Selah means *pause and think about it.* Let's just do that right now.

- His blessing is *upon* me.
- What does that look like?
- What does it feel like?
- How do I act if that is true?
- What is my thought life if that is true?
- What does the future hold if His blessing is upon His people?

Now look at the following verses:

> And all these blessings shall come upon you and
> overtake you, because you obey the voice of the
> Lord your God.
>
> ———— Deuteronomy 28:2 ————

> Blessings are on the head of the righteous, but
> violence covers the mouth of the wicked.
>
> ———— Proverbs 10:6 ————

> For You, O Lord, will bless the righteous; with
> favor You will surround him as with a shield.
>
> ———— Psalm 5:12 ————

DAY 17

LOOK FOR SOMEONE TO BLESS

On the first day, we learned the Hebrew word for blessing is *barak*. From the root word *barak* comes another word *berakah*. It means:

- Source of blessing
- Blessing, prosperity
- Blessing, praise of God
- A gift, present
- Blessing, benediction, invocation of good
- Benediction of favor of God, the result of which is prosperity and good of every kind
- The blessing of good, but more often benefits, gifts divinely bestowed
- Extremely fortunate and happy

Understanding of this Hebrew word comes from Deuteronomy 16:17 (KJV):

> *Every man shall give as he is able, according to the blessing of the LORD thy God which he hath given thee.*

God has blessed us so we get to be a source of blessing to others— make them blessed, peaceful, and happy.

We are blessed to be a blessing! God told Abraham, "I will make you a great nation; I will bless you and make your name great; and you shall be a blessing" (Genesis 12:2).

It is said of Abraham and Sarah that their tent was always open, meaning they were always looking for ways to bless others. They wanted to see, so they could show kindness and generosity. The open tent signified being open to others. With this as their motivation, they blessed:

- Melchizedek

- Lot

- Angels

- Abimelech

We are sent with the blessing of the Lord and the blessing of Abraham (Galatians 3:9, 29); therefore, we can be a blessing no matter what our situation! We don't wait until_____ (fill in the blank with your excuse for not giving), but we bless according to the blessing God has given us right now.

In I Samuel 30 we read where David had gone through a difficult time. He had returned to Ziklag from battle and found his family taken and all he had burned, as well as every one of his fighting men's families and possessions. They all wanted to stone him, but God said go and recover all—and that is what he did. When he returned, what did he do? He blessed all his friends with the spoils of the enemy—a gift of blessing!

Now when David came to Ziklag, he sent some of the spoil to the elders of Judah, to his friends, saying, "Here is a present for you from the spoil of the enemies of the Lord."

1 Samuel 30:26

MEDITATION:

Reread the preceeding scriptures.

Declare: "I am blessed to be a blessing."

We are to give according to the blessing that is on our lives as stated in Deuteronomy 16:17. Ask the Lord how you can be a blessing right now to people in your life through a gift.

DAY 18
CONFIDENT

Are you confident of God's blessing? We see Abraham's confidence on full display when he charged his closest servant to find a wife for his son Isaac. Even though his servant responded in doubt, unbelief, and fear, Abraham boldly told him:

> *The Lord God of heaven, who took me from my father's house and from the land of my family, and who spoke to me and swore to me, saying, 'To your descendant I give this land,' He will send His angel before you, and you shall take a wife for my son from there.*
>
> *Genesis 24:7*

The confidence Abraham walked in came from his belief that he and his family were blessed. His belief and obedience to the promises of God on his life set a course that made overcoming the impossible an ordinary occurrence. Most of the hard times in our lives come from trying to fulfill the promises of God in our own strength. Obedience will always keep us on the path of fulfilled promises.

Through obedience, Abraham stepped into the blessing of the Lord. His path was set. The future of his family line was certain. Abraham knew with confidence that if he couldn't go find a wife for Isaac, then the Lord would send an angel to give him success. Not only that, but God promised to bless those that blessed him, so why should his servant worry? Of course he'd be successful in finding a wife for Isaac! And he was! The first girl Abraham's servant met turned out to be Rebekah!

And he said, "Blessed be the Lord God of my master Abraham, who has not forsaken His mercy and His truth toward my master. As for me, being on the way, the Lord led me to the house of my master's brethren."

Genesis 24:27

And I bowed my head and worshiped the Lord, and blessed the Lord God of my master Abraham, who had led me in the way of truth to take the daughter of my master's brother for his son.

Genesis 24:48

Today, make a choice to surrender your doubt, unbelief, and fear to the Father. These things are rooted in a belief that our success is solely up to us and our own capabilities. What a scary proposition. The truth is we will never walk in confidence by trying to accomplish the call of God on our life in our own strength.

Begin to dream with God again. What has He called you to do? What is He declaring over you? No matter how big or small take daily steps of obedience. It will always lead you to the blessed path—where promises are fulfilled—and you will grow in confidence that will impact a generation.

MEDITATION:

Read the full story of Abraham, his servant, and Rebekah in Genesis 24.

Notice how bold and confident Abraham is, not out of arrogance or pride, but out of trust and assurance in the blessing.

Take note of how that confidence is released to others and how their lives change because of it.

Ask the Lord for this kind of trust to arise for your future because of your assurance in the blessing.

Listen to the *Declarative Prayer* on CD or read it on page 6 and allow confidence to emerge in your prayer life.

DAY 19
A CHANGED MINDSET

A braham took God at His Word because He is not a man that He should lie. God said it, he believed it, and that settled it. He had unwavering confidence in the character and nature of God. Therefore, His Word could be trusted. He lived life and journeyed with God with complete expectation that good things were going to happen *to* him and *for* him because of the blessing.

> I will make you a great nation; I will bless you and make your name great; and you shall be a blessing. I will bless those who bless you, and I will curse him who curses you; and in you all the families of the earth shall be blessed.
>
> *Genesis 12:2-3*

Those around him saw the blessing and wanted it. Freely he gave it away because he was so blessed he knew more would come back to him (Genesis 13:6-12). He had a generous mindset that said, *Everyone on earth is going to be blessed by me. How can I make that happen today?* Abraham and Sarah looked for ways to bless others.

Do you live in that same place of generosity and overflow, or do you often view people and circumstances as a means to get what you want or need? We can easily slip into a poverty mindset, viewing the world through eyes of lack, hoping they will fulfill something missing in us. Walking in the reality of the Father's blessing will completely change your mindset. What if you began to realize you hold the answers to the problems existing all around you? Christ in *you*, the hope of glory! (Colossians 1:27) You would no longer seek out others from a place of lack or need for fulfillment, instead you would seize opportunities to bring life to everyone you encounter.

Walking in the Father's blessing also removes our need to *get even*, or make things *fair*. Assured in the blessing of the Lord, Abraham wasn't afraid of being taken advantage of, or things not going his way. He was not swayed by circumstances. If someone took advantage of him, the blessing would take care of it. He understood God would bless those that blessed him and curse those that cursed him. His job was to obey. God is faithful and just and is our defender.

> *Do not repay evil for evil or reviling for reviling, but on the contrary blessing, for to this you were called, that you may obtain a blessing.*
>
> 1 Peter 3:9

Jesus preached this mindset change in the Sermon on the Mount. He exhorted the multitude in Kingdom perspective when He declared we were to:

> *...love your enemies, bless those who curse you, do good to those who hate you, and pray for those who spitefully use you and persecute you, that you may be sons of your Father in heaven...*
>
> Matthew 5:44-45

May you be fully aware of the blessing on your life today. Being fully aware of the Father's blessing will greatly expand your perception of what is possible with Him.

MEDITATION:

How confident are you in God's ability to take care of *everything* in your life? Are there areas where you are distrustful, doubting, or insecure?

Repent of fear and look with new eyes of faith at the path set before you that is blessed. God knelt down and spoke everything you need.

Do the opposite of fear—if you have been worried over your finances—give some away.

If you have been afraid of messing up—do it anyway. You can't mess up.

If you have been afraid of the future—step out!

DAY 20

DEATH AND LIFE

As God spoke the blessing over us, His children, He bent down and made our path straight. Our course is true and our foundation is strong. What a tremendous privilege and honor He has bestowed on us by the power and potency of His spoken Word.

But wait, there's more! Just when we thought it couldn't get any better, we find out He gives us the power to bless others too! Through our words we have the ability to affect the lives of those around us.

Death and life are in the power of the tongue, and those who love it will eat its fruits.

Proverbs 18:21

Our words are powerful. They can be used to build up or tear down. We can set hearts free or strengthen the chains that surround them. The Father has given our words the power to transform lives, and we must remember that every person we encounter is important to Him.

Because we are the children of our Heavenly Father, it is important we begin to talk and act like Him. You have *received* the blessing—you are blessed. Therefore, you can bless others. One of the greatest opportunities we have to speak blessings is within our own family. Husbands blessing wives, wives blessing husbands, parents blessing their children (Ephesians 5:22-6:4). Blessing your family on a regular basis keeps the reality of their God-given, God-spoken identity in the forefront of their mind, and helps nurture the same confidence you have found in receiving the Father's blessing. Let's face it, we live in a society that is not reinforcing who we are in Christ. In fact, most of the time, the world is painting quite the opposite picture. Words of blessing and remembrance are crucial to strengthening the core of our families.

There are several key times in Scripture when man blesses:

BIRTH

> *So it was, on the eighth day, that they came to circumcise the child; and they would have called him by the name of his father, Zacharias. His mother answered and said, "No; he shall be called John."*
>
> Luke 1:59-60

MARRIAGE

> *And they blessed Rebekah and said to her: "Our sister, may you become The mother of thousands of ten thousands; and may your descendants possess The gates of those who hate them."*
>
> Genesis 24:60

A JOURNEY

> *And early in the morning Laban rose up, and kissed his sons and his daughters, and blessed them: and Laban departed, and returned unto his place.*
>
> Genesis 31:55

PARENT'S DEATH BED

*By faith Jacob, when he was dying, blessed each of the
sons of Joseph, and worshiped, leaning on the top of
his staff.*

Hebrews 11:21

Jewish communities all over the world have put into practice two
other times to bless:

God called the seventh day blessed, so Jews observe weekly
Sabbath. It is a time to rest, study Scripture, starting with a
family meal where the father blesses the mother and children.

At coming of age (thirteen for boys and twelve for girls), a
special ceremony is given to commemorate the time and release a
blessing. These are called *bar mitzvah* and *bat mitzvah*.

Learn to begin to speak and release the blessing, and see how
straight, happy, and prosperous your families' lives become.

MEDITATION:

Take a few minutes to meditate on Proverbs 18:21.

Think about the words you speak over yourself, and
others. Are there negative words (curses) you need to stop
saying? Are there positive words (blessings) you need to
declare more often?

Read over the preceeding verses where man blessed others.

Do you have any of the above opportunities coming up soon?
A birth, marriage, etc., where you could release a blessing?

Pray and ask the Lord to give you a short one-sentence blessing you can speak over each of your family members this week on Sabbath. Write down what He says to speak over them.

Listen to *Blessing and Cursing* on CD or read it on page 8.

DAY 21
POWER OF YOUR WORDS

In the Book of Numbers, there is an interesting story of a gifted man named Balaam. His gift was in his mouth. He had the power to bless and to curse. He had a spiritual gift, but he used it for the enemy. The enemy has been using this tactic for thousands of years—to use the gifts of God *that are* without repentance (Romans 11:29) for himself—look at Hitler. Balaam clearly had a leadership gift, yet he used it for evil. He spoke with God. God visited him and talked to him. He had angels come to him. Despite all of these gifts, Balaam used his mouth for divination.

We have gifts and callings just like Balaam. We get to choose every day who we will serve, and which Father we will sound like—Father God or the Father of Lies (John 8:43-45).

A good man out of the good treasure of his heart brings forth good things, and an evil man out of the evil treasure brings forth evil things. But I say to you that for every idle word men may speak, they will give account of it in the day of judgment. For by your words you will be justified, and by your words you will be condemned.

Matthew 12:35-37

Our mouths have power and we have to be careful what we say! They can be used to build up or tear down. We can set hearts free or strengthen the chains surrounding them. The Father has given our words power to transform lives, and we must remember every person we encounter is important to Him. The young man working the local drive-through window, the teller at the bank, or the person bagging our groceries—each of them is valuable to the Father. The people we interact with every day are our assignment for the day. What are we speaking over their lives? Life or death?

Charles Capps once posed the question, *What if everything we said came true?* Think about that! "You are so stupid!" "I'm sick and tired." Or worse.

James tells us we set a course for our lives kindled by Hell if we aren't on alert:

> *Even so the tongue is a little member and boasts great things. See how great a forest a little fire kindles! And the tongue is a fire, a world of iniquity. The tongue is so set among our members that it defiles the whole body, and sets on fire the course of nature; and it is set on fire by hell... With it we bless our God and Father, and with it we curse men, who have been made in the similitude of God. Out of the same mouth proceed blessing and cursing. My brethren, these things ought not to be so. Does a spring send forth fresh water and bitter from the same opening? Can a fig tree, my brethren, bear olives, or a grapevine bear figs? Thus no spring yields both salt water and fresh.*

> James 3: 5-6; 9-12

> ## MEDITATION:
>
> Listen to *Blessing and Cursing* on CD or read it on page 8—just taking it in.
>
> What is the Holy Spirit saying to you?
>
> Choose this day to use the gift in your mouth to bless God and others.

ABOUT THE AUTHORS

Joshua and Jodi Young have a passion to see others discover and fulfill the purpose for which they were created. Throughout the years they have functioned in the roles of worship leader, pastor, and teacher—encouraging and inspiring others to explore the wide-open spaces of the Father's heart. Traveling extensively throughout the U.S. and abroad, they have a heart to equip others to search out and walk in the ways of God. Joshua is the director of Streams Music and has released several worship CDs through Streams Ministries. Jodi wrote and developed *The Art of Hearing God for Kids*. These teachings and other resources can be found at www.streamsministries. com, or their personal website www.joshuaandjodiyoung.com.

ABOUT STREAMS

OUR FOUNDER

John Paul Jackson dedicated his life to passionately pursuing God and His mysteries. The results were books, teachings, courses, and a groundbreaking TV program, all of which will stand the test of time as some of the most relevant and spirit-provoking Christian teaching of our day.

OUR MISSION

Streams Ministries is an equipping ministry that offers spiritual teaching and media designed to help you hear God, reveal the often overlooked ways in which God speaks, and train and empower believers at all levels of spiritual maturity to begin using their gifts to spread the truth and power of the gospel.

REVEALING GOD

Whether you're a lifelong Christian or just someone interested in starting a spiritual journey of discovery, change doesn't begin until God becomes real to you. We believe God is speaking to us all the time, but some of us simply aren't hearing His voice. First and foremost, our teaching, resources, TV and film projects are focused on revealing the awe and supernatural presence of God to every generation.

AWAKENING DREAMS

Once you discover God is real and present in your everyday life, you also realize He has a unique plan on earth just for you.

Our desire is to call forth that unique destiny by helping you align the dreams and aspirations of your heart with the Creator who put them there. We offer courses and workshops focused on practical training to help you reach the purpose for which you were created.

CHANGING LIVES

We're not just interested in changing your life; our vision and goal are to teach and inspire you so you can change others' lives as well. Our training and resources will draw the surface and sharpen the gifts God has given you, which, once matured, can be used to help others do the same.

**To learn more about the resources
and online courses we offer from
John Paul Jackson and others, please visit
our website at streamsministries.com.
Or call us at 1.888.441.8080.**

THE ART OF HEARING GOD FOR KIDS

BY JODI YOUNG

The Art of Hearing God for Kids curriculum is designed to teach your 1st to 6th-grader how to recognize and obey God's voice through 18 Bible-based, activity-packed lessons.

OTHER BOOKS BY
STREAMS MINISTRIES AND
JOHN PAUL JACKSON

Several of these titles are also available on most e-reader formats. To find them, open your favorite e-reader app such as iBooks, Kindle, NOOK, etc. and enter "John Paul Jackson".

CLASS IS IN SESSION!

WITH JOHN PAUL JACKSON'S
ONLINE CLASSROOM

Take any of our six university-caliber courses written and taught
by John Paul Jackson. It's never been easier to take a quantum leap
forward in your spiritual walk. Each of these 23-hour courses can be
streamed right to your computer, tablet, or smartphone.

Begin your journey to understand all God has for you by going to
StreamsMinistries.com.
Click on "Online Classroom."